TITHING:
WHAT DOES GOD REQUIRE?

TITHING:
WHAT DOES GOD REQUIRE?

A LAYMAN'S BIBLICAL
REFERENCE GUIDE
ON TITHING AND GIVING

By
Fredrick Douglas Richardson, Jr.

Bethlehem Book Publishers, Inc.
2415 Twelfth Avenue South
Nashville, TN 37204
1999

TITHING: WHAT DOES GOD REQUIRE?

© 1996 by Fredrick D. Richardson

Published by:
Bethlehem Book Publishers, Inc.
2415 Twelfth Avenue South, Nashville, TN 37204
(615) 463-8642 Corp.Off.
(615) 463-8643 FAX
E-mail: bethlehm@bellsouth.net
www.bethbooksinc.com

Cover Design: Bryan Lewis
Layout: Pavel Bukengolts

All Rights Reserved

No portion of this book may be reproduced without
written permission from the author and/or publisher.

Printed in the United States of America

ISBN: 0-927618-11-7
LOC: 99-94355

DEDICATION

I am dedicating this book to my three children: **LaWanda**, **Lisa** and **Fredrick III**; and to my two grand children, **Crystal** and **Maya**. It is my hope that after each of them has completely read this book, valuable insight will be gained on the subject of **Tithing.** At the same time, I TRUST they will discover the tools for effective study listed herein: Tools that are necessary to supply them all the elements needed to enjoy a lifetime of Bible study.

CONTENTS

INTRODUCTION

It is suggested that before you start reading this treatise or exposition (facts and principles which serve as a basis for reaching a final conclusion), you should have by your side the only document used to examine the subject of **TITHING**: The Holy Bible, as translated from the Authorized King James Version (KJV). Get your Bible and we are off.

The purpose for writing this book was to hopefully dispel commonly believed false teachings regarding God's requirement for giving financial gifts. Does HE, or does HE not require each Christian to give ten percent of **money** earned to the church? That is the question I expect to answer, hopefully to your satisfaction. Certainly it will be answered in light of The Word. When you finish reading this book I trust your knowledge will be enhanced and expanded to the extent that your confidence and understanding in The Word is reinforced. It is understood that those who have already taught false doctrine regarding **tithing** will have a difficult time changing, especially pastors. It is better to be right than to look good.

Without a doubt, many readers will have their belief system challenged regarding **TITHING**. You, the reader, will have the task of accepting the conclusion or rejecting it. It is hoped that whatever decision you make in reaching a conclusion, you will use scripture to support your belief. For in the final analysis, Gospel is what the Bible says; and gossip is what someone else says.

Certainly the time has come for the whole issue of **TITH-ING** to come to the fore-front for examination by all who feel, either that there is no such requirement for believers in the church today; or by those who feel to do so is not only right, but is required by GOD for all who believe.

When the reader has finished this layman's manual or handbook on **Tithing**, this writer does not expect that person to give any more or less to the church. What the writer expects is that the reader will know the truth from fiction; to the extent that giving will become a thing of joy, having been set free by the truth. To God be the Glory. **AMEN**.

Fredrick Douglas Richardson, Jr. (1995)

ACKNOWLEDGEMENTS

I take this opportunity to acknowledge and graciously express many thanks to my able and capable text scrutinizer, Mrs. Karen Burrows Pontius, for the laborious and competent job she did in assuring the perpetuation of word accuracy for this manuscript.

CHAPTER ONE

GETTING READY TO STUDY
THE BIBLE: TOOLS AND RULES

There are basic rules to follow when one studies the Holy Bible. To disregard the rules may well lead one to a false conclusion regarding the subject matter you are researching. It was the Prophet **Isaiah** who spelled out the rules of studying in **chapter 28** of his book, **verses 9 and 10**, when he stated:

9. Whom shall he teach knowledge? and whom shall he make to understand doctrine? Them that are weaned from milk, and drawn from the breasts.

10. For precept must be upon precept, precept upon precept; line upon line, line upon line; here a little, and there a little.

It is clear from the scripture above that once you have a definite subject matter to research, the next move is that of searching the Bible for all related scripture touching on that subject matter (*"here a little, and there a little"*).

Once you have explored all Biblical references on the subject you are researching (*"line upon line"*), only then are you in a position to formulate a particular belief regarding the subject you are studying.

Committing one verse to memory on a subject which has many biblical references and holding that one verse as a basis for your belief could (more likely than not) lead you to a false conclusion. We must study in order to find the truth. **Paul** told Timothy to:

15. Study to shew thyself approved unto GOD, a workman that needeth not to be ashamed, rightly dividing the word of truth (II Timothy 2:15 emphasis mine, KJV).

Another rule for studying the Bible: If there are times when it seems the Bible has contradicted itself, please consider the problem to be your own misunderstanding of the scriptures. Pray, at this point, that God will open your medium of understanding. As our beloved brother **Paul** wrote to the Romans: *"Let God be true, but every man a liar...." (Romans 3:4a, KJV)*.

As a matter of practice, let us study briefly a subject we will refer to as **THE LAW**, as an example to test your belief system on this subject. We will review a common Christian belief regarding **THE LAW** as a basis to show the importance of conducting scriptural research, in every instance, before establishing a belief on any subject.

This statement is commonly made by Christians: *WE ARE NOT UNDER THE LAW. WE ARE UNDER GRACE*. Was it not Jesus Himself who reminded us to:

17. Think not that I am come to destroy the LAW, or the prophets: I am not come to destroy, but to fulfill.

18. For verily I say unto you, till heaven and earth pass, one jot or one tittle shall in no wise pass from the LAW till all be fulfilled (Matthew 5:17-18 emphasis mine, KJV).

James, in his epistle, told us:

"If ye fulfill the royal LAW according to the scripture, thou shalt love thy neighbour as thyself, ye do well. But if ye have respect to persons, ye commit sin, and are convinced of the LAW as transgressors. For whosoever shall keep the whole LAW, and yet offend in one point, he is guilty of all" (James 2:8-10 emphasis mine, KJV).

*Paul, in writing to the **Romans** stated of the LAW:*

12. Wherefore the LAW is holy, and the commandment holy, and just, and good (Romans 7:12 emphasis mine, KJV).

In the book of **Psalms, Number 19,** David makes the statement that:

7. The LAW of the Lord is perfect... (Psalm 19:7a emphasis mine, KJV).

Even the prophet **Nehemiah** spoke of the Law when he stated:

13. Thou camest down also upon mount Sinai, and spakest with them from heaven, and gavest them right judgments, and true Laws, good statutes and commandments (Nehemiah 9:13 KJV).

As we get ready to study, let us look at what appears to be a drastic contradiction to all of the above references which, without a doubt, highlighted the fact that we are still under God's **LAW.**

The Apostle Paul, in his letter to the churches in **Galatia**, made this statement:

Wherefore the Law was our schoolmaster to bring us unto Christ, that we might be justified by faith. But after that faith is come, we are no longer under a schoolmaster (Galatians 3:24-25, KJV).

In the fifth (5th) chapter of the same book, **Paul** went on to say to the churches in **Galatia**:

But if ye be led of the Spirit, ye are not under the Law (Galatians, 5:18 KJV).

This same **Paul**, when he wrote to churches at Rome told them:

...For where no Law is, there is no transgression (Romans 4:15, KJV).

On the one hand, seemingly Paul is saying, in **Romans 4:15b**, that where there is no Law, then one cannot be charged with doing wrong. In other words, in order for God to call each of us up before **HIM** on the day of final judgment, to judge us for deeds done in the flesh, there must first be a **Law** against such deeds. This being true, why would Paul write that we are not under the **Law**? The answer lies in the fact that there was more than one **Law**. We have **God's Law**: The Ten (10) Commandments; and we have the **Law of Moses**.

So then, the confusion comes when Christians fail to realize that there were two **Laws**: God's Law and Moses **Law**. One ended with the crucifixion of Jesus, Moses **LAW** (*see Colossians 2:13-14*) and the other **LAW** remains (God's **LAW**). Paul realized this when he was writing to the various churches.

Such confusion in not getting the proper understanding was stressed by Peter when making reference to Paul's writings when he stated:

...Even as our beloved brother Paul also according to the wisdom given unto him hath written unto you; As also in all his epistles, speaking in them of these things; in which are some things hard to be understood, which they that are unlearned and unstable wrest, as they do also the other scriptures, unto their own destruction (II Peter 3:15b-16).

What of this other **Law** that ended with the death of Jesus: The **Law of Moses**? The scripture is loaded with references regarding the **Law of Moses**.

First of all, **Moses' Law** was written in a book, while **God's Law** was written on two tables of stone, by God Himself *(Exodus 32:15-16).* From the book of **Deuteronomy** (one of the five [5] books of Moses) we find these words:

And it came to pass, when Moses had made an end of writing the words of this Law in a book, until they were finished, that Moses commanded the Levites, which bare the ark of the covenant of the Lord, saying, take this Book of the Law, and put it in the side of the ark of the covenant of the Lord your God, that it may be there for a witness against thee (Deuteronomy 31:24-26 KJV).

God authored His own **Law** on two tables of stone, not in a book as Moses did. When He finished writing it Moses was called into the mountain to meet God and receive the **Law** of Commandments:

And the Lord said unto Moses, come up to me into the mount, and be there: And I will give thee tables of stone, and a Law, and commandments which I have written; that thou mayest teach them (Exodus 24:12 KJV).

So important was God's **Law** that after Moses, out of anger, broke the tables of stone, he was called back into the mountain where God had rewritten His **Law**. **Moses** said:

And it came to pass at the end of forty days and forty nights, that the Lord gave me the two tables of stone, even the tables of the covenant (Deuteronomy 9:11 KJV).

If you read the two verses prior to verse 11 you will find that God wrote His **Law** with His own finger.

Again, the paradox, that is, what appeared to be a contradiction, only required additional reading in order to obtain a better understanding regarding The **Law**.

In his letter to the **Galatians**, Paul made it clear he was writing of "**Things which are written in the book of the Law**" (Gal. 3:10b, KJV). Who wrote his **Law** in a book? Moses wrote his **Law** in a book. Remember, God wrote His Law with His own finger on two tables of stone.

When writing to the **Colossians**, **Paul** made it clear the **Law** he wrote of, which came to an end, was written in "handwriting" (**Moses Law**). He wrote to them:

Blotting out the handwriting of ordinances that was against us which was contrary to us, and took it out of the way, nailing it to His cross (Colossians 2:14, emphasis mine, KJV).

It is clear the **Apostle Paul** made reference above to Moses' **Law**. Moses' **Law** provided instruction for sinners to receive forgiveness. The atonement process is spelled out in great detail in the book of **Leviticus**, starting with chapter one. However, when Jesus was crucified, the veil of the temple was rent (split), indicating an end of the **Law** of Moses which dealt with the process of atoning. Only the priest could make sacrifices at the altar. According to **Matthew**, when Jesus was crucified the holy veil, that separated worshipers from the high priest, was rent (ripped apart) from top to bottom:

And, behold, the veil of the temple was rent in twain from the top to the bottom... (Matthew 27:51a, KJV).

The meaning was man should no longer be separated from God by the High Priest. Only Jesus can come between man and God today. Even Jesus made reference to the **Law of Moses** when he said:

If a man on the Sabbath day receive circumcision, that the Law of Moses should not be broken; are ye angry at me, because I have made a man every whit whole on the Sabbath day? (John 7:23, KJV).

This chapter had little of nothing to do with the question of **Tithing**. The goal was to address the issue regarding the proper way to study the Bible, especially when approaching a complicated issue such as **Tithing**. Stick with instructions given in *Isaiah 28: 9-10* as to how to study and you will not be led wrong. Don't base your belief on one verse in the Bible. Get the whole picture before forming a belief. Don't be afraid to change when you are convinced, through studying the scripture, your former belief was unfounded.

It is desired that you found the above exercise helpful. For sure, the next few chapters will challenge your thinking as well as your beliefs: Be prepared to defend them both. Let the Bible be true, even when you don't understand. Never fall for vain philosophy of men as **Paul** has already warned:

Beware lest any man spoil you through philosophy and vain deceit (Colossians 2:8).

Always remember, God can and will, at times, hide it from the wise and reveal it unto babes (*Matthew 11:25*). Talk to other believers regarding issues unclear to you. Just don't forget to use the rules you learned. Also, don't be afraid to ask: "Where in the Bible can I find what you just told me"? Just say you need to study that scripture for yourself. Remember, gossip is what they say: Gospel is what the Bible says.

CHAPTER TWO

FAULTY POPULAR BELIEFS ABOUT TITHING .

This chapter will be devoted to shedding light on faulty popular beliefs about **Tithing**. Many Christians will state their belief in **Tithing**; but beyond **Malachi 3:8-10**, they have no further basis for keeping the tradition. Many, with the strongest beliefs in **Tithing**, fail to practice what they preach. They only argue what they believe, not thus said The Word.

The matter of **Tithing** becomes most important when the supposition (something that is supposed) is added which infers that God Himself requires of us ten percent of our income (money earned or otherwise received). And further, not to give it to Him (the percent) is to rob Him: And for robbing Him, God will cause harm to come your way. I find no scripture to support this supposition. As a matter of fact, I challenge you to find the word **"earn"** or **"earnings"** in the scriptures.

The prophet **Micah**, in no uncertain terms, told us what God requires and he never mentioned **Tithing** as a requirement. This is what **Micah** had to say:

He hath shewed thee, O man, what is good; and what doth the Lord require of thee, but to do justly, and love mercy, and to walk humbly with thy God? (Micah 6:8, KJV).

Moses extolled (praise highly) Israel seven hundred years before the prophet **Micah** made the statement above, to do as God had commanded. He made clear God's requirement when he had this to say:

And now Israel, what doth the Lord thy God require of thee, but to fear the Lord thy God, to walk in all His ways, and to love Him, and to serve the Lord thy God with all thy heart and with all thy soul, to keep the Commandments of the Lord, and his statutes, which I command thee this day for thy good? (Deuteronomy 10:12-13, KJV).

Solomon, in the book of **Ecclesiastes**, affirmed the words above when he wrote:

Let us hear the conclusion of the whole matter: Fear God, and keep His commandments: For this is the WHOLE DUTY of man (Ecclesiastes, Chapter 12:13).

The Bible is crystal clear on what God requires and it is not ten percent of your salary or paycheck. The church was not commissioned to raise **money** for God; but to save souls. The great commission as stated in *Matthew 28:19-20* made absolutely no reference to **money**. The church's mission is to go, and *"teach all nations" (vs. 19).*

Jesus told the Apostles to teach "*them to observe all things whatsoever I have commanded you" (vs 20)*. If Jesus taught **Tithing** to the Apostles, I believe they would have taught the same to the early church. We have no Biblical record that any of the Apostles ever uttered the word. The apostles understood the Great Commission. **Tithing** was not a part of the New Testament teaching.

It is important to note here that not one of the Apostles preached a message on **Tithing** that the scriptures recorded. The scriptures failed to show where any of them even mentioned the word **Tithing.** Do you suppose they forgot to mention it? Don't you think one of the twelve (12) apostles would have reminded the saints of their duty to give God ten percent of what they earned, had that actually been a requirement? We must answer that question with a resounding **YES!!!!!**

Don't you know that if **Tithing** had played an important role in the plan of salvation Jesus would have taught the subject to his disciples? Well, if you believe that one can go to hell for not giving ten percent, you also believe **Tithing** plays an important role in the plan of salvation. You better be careful when you add to God's word.

Jesus only mentioned the subject once, only to condemn the action of scribes and pharisees as hypocrites who payed **tithe** of **MINT** (plant of spice), **ANISE** (plant of spice) and **CUMMIN** (plant of spice as recorded in *Isaiah 28:25-27*). Jesus Said:

Woe unto you scribes and pharisees, hypocrites! For ye pay (the word **PAY** led many to think incorrectly that Jesus' reference was to **MONEY**) **tithe of MINT** (look up this word) **and ANISE** (look up this word also) **and CUMMIN** (look this word up also)**, and have omitted the weightier matters of the law; judgment, mercy, and faith: These ought ye to have done and not to leave the other undone (Matthew 23:23, emphasis mine, KJV).**

Actually, those religious leaders were cited by Jesus as paying **tithe**. They paid in food related materials as was required. "**Mint**" and "**Anise**" and "**Cummin**" all were food related and came from plants. Luke quoted Jesus as He cited the same passage of scripture when he said:

But woe unto you, Pharisees! For ye TITHE mint and rue AND ALL MANNER OF HERBS (Luke 11:42, emphasis mine).

The Pharisees paid their **TITHE** in all manner of food and spices . This would have been a great opportunity for Jesus to condemn church leaders for not giving ten percent of their earnings to the church. Yet, he said not a word regarding their **money** when mentioning the **tithe**.

Surely we can't reason they had no **money**, as some do. The treasury was where **money** at the church or temple was kept. In **Matthew 27:6** we find these words:

And the chief priests took the silver pieces, and said, it is not lawful for to put them into the treasury, because it is the price of blood.

The 30 pieces were paid to Judas.

On another occasion, Jesus *"sat over against the TREASURY, and beheld how the people cast MONEY into the TREASURY: And many that were rich cast much" (Mark 12:41, emphasis mine, KJV).*

Yes, even in Jesus' time **money** was placed in the **TREASURY**, while they still brought the **Tithe** in the form of food, to the **STOREHOUSE**.

When Jesus stated *"these ought ye to have done,"* in *Matthew 23:23,* he meant their food substance was proper to pay as **tithe: Money** would have been improper. You see, those vegetables, herbs and spices cited in **Matthew 23:23** were used both as food and to savor cooked food, thereby enhancing the taste and smell.

As we examine the subject of **Tithing** maybe the word itself should be looked at first. The Greek word for **Tithing** is dekatos=δεκατος (meaning tenth). So, we can ascertain the fact that to give a **Tithe** was to give a tenth (10th). The question now is, a tenth (10th) of what? The Bible only should answer that question for us. Only God Himself is qualified to describe what actually constitutes a **tithe.** On more than one occasion God did just that.

We will get to that later.

This could be the perfect time to review the most popular verse in the Bible on the subject of **Tithing**: *Malachi 3:8-10*, which states:

Will a man rob God? Yet ye have robbed me. But ye say, wherein have we robbed thee? In TITHES and offerings. Ye are cursed with a curse: For ye have robbed me, even this whole nation. Bring ye all the TITHES into the storehouse, that there may be meat in mine house, and prove me now herewith, saith the Lord of hosts, if I will not open you the windows of heaven, and pour you out a blessing, that there shall not be room enough to receive it (Malachi 3:8-10, emphasis mine, KJV).

Often when we see the word "**ROB**," we equate the word with someone who unjustly removes valuables from another, such as **money** or jewelry. **Malachi** was burdened with the word from God, to tell the priests, God's messengers, how they had robbed God. Let us look in the first chapter of his book and see how God was robbed:

Vs 6. A son honoureth his father, and a servant his master: if then I be a father, where is my honour? And if I be a master, where is my fear? saith the Lord of hosts unto you, O priests, that despise my name. And ye say, wherein have we despised thy name?

Vs. 7. Ye offer polluted bread upon mine altar; and ye say, wherein have we polluted thee? In that ye say, the table of the Lord is contemptible.

Vs. 8. And ye offer the blind for sacrifice, is it not evil? And if ye offer the lame and sick, is it not evil? offer it now unto thy governor; will he be pleased with thee, or accept thy person? saith the Lord of hosts (Malachi 1:6-8 KJV).

The problem was not that God had lost any **money** to robbers, the problem in the above scripture was that God's servants, the priests, had offered to God what they knew was unacceptable, and expected a blessing. God wanted the first-lings or the first one and the unblemished, not the sick and lame for a sacrificial offering. Yes, when they kept the best for themselves and gave God the absolute worse, they surely robbed Him.

Matters get worse in chapter two. Again it is clear that the priests mentioned in **Malachi** had robbed God by keeping for themselves the good healthy animals and food, which were placed at the temple for an offering to God. In exchange, the priests offered to God, the sick, lame and polluted animals (**Malachi 1:7-8**). Nowhere is it suggested by **Malachi** that God was robbed because He did not receive all the **money** He was entitled to receive. That idea was made up by persons seeking **money**.

All of the gold and **silver** already belongs to the Lord (**Haggai 2:8**). Those priests were suppose to bring only the best to the Lord; animals *"without blemish"* (**Leviticus 1:3**). Additionally, a tenth of what they received from the other tribes were to be offered to God as a sacrifice:

Thus speak unto the Levites, and say unto them, when ye take of the children of Israel the TITHES, which I have given you from them for your inheritance, then ye shall offer up an heave-offering of it for the Lord, EVEN A TENTH PART OF THE TITHE (Numbers 18:26, em-phasis mine). You see, they robbed God when they refused to give back a tenth part of the **Tithe**. God got only the re-fused.

It was against the law to tax the priests for **money**. **Money** was given to them but they could not be forced to give **money** back to the sanctuary. But from the scripture in **Numbers 18:26** it clearly indicated a tenth of their **tithe** was to be given back as an offering.

From the book of **Ezra** it was made clear *"...the priests, Levites, singers, porters, Nethinims, or ministers* *of this house of God, IT SHALL NOT BE LAWFUL TO IMPOSE TOLL, TRIBUTE, OR CUSTOM, UPON THEM" (Ezra 7:24, emphasis mine).*

The point being, when it came to food, which was received in the form of **tithe**, the Levites or priests had to give back ten percent of what they received. On the other hand, when it came to **money**, the Levites or priests could not be taxed; proving **tithe** and **money** were not the same.

Back to the book of **Malachi.**

I hope you know by now the book of **Malachi** is in no way about **money**. On the contrary, that book is about insincere and dishonest religious leaders who knew better, but went on to hood-wink and deceive the congregation of God's people; all in the name of the Lord. They demanded only the best from the congregation, but they themselves gave God their refuse and garbage, in the form of sick, blind and lame animals. This kind of deception is alive and well in all too many of our churches today. The stakes are raised high when it comes to the congregation. But when it comes to church leaders, performance in the area of giving often fall short. In many instances those in charge collecting and counting **money** in the church give the least. Thus was the story of the priest.

Some churches teach another doctrine, that an **"OFFERING"** is all you pay above ten percent. There is no Biblical evidence to support such teaching. It sounds good but lacks a scriptural foundation. "Offering" derived from the root word *offer,* and it refers to what one gives as a freewill gift. It has to do with whatever you offer. It has nothing to do with more or less ten percent. Some person threw in that phrase to conjure extra **money** from the saints.

The idea was that God wants ten percent of what you give. But the church wants the offering which is all above ten percent. Such teaching has no scriptural foundation. Again, Gospel is what the Bible says, gossip is what you or someone else say. If you are being told the same thing regarding the offering, ask for scriptural references.

Look at the **first chapter of Leviticus** for documentation. What ever you offer to God, your time or **money**, if it comes from the heart it will be accepted. What is offered to God has nothing to do with **Tithing**.

Let us come back to the popular verses on tithing. **Malachi 3:10** is a good place to start:

"Bring ye all the TITHE into the storehouse...."(Vs.10a). What was the "**storehouse**"? Was it a place to store **money**? What is clear is that the **TITHE** should be placed into the "**storehouse**". God instructed the Israelites to eat out of the "**STORE**" until fruit was gathered (**Leviticus 25:19-22**).

Clearly the **STORE or STOREHOUSE** was not built to house **money** but to house processed food. If, at this point you feel you know why the Israelites were bringing food to the **storehouse**, then I say hold all your supporting scripture. If you couldn't find any to support your belief, change it.

For your review, I will list below all scriptural references to **STORE, STOREHOUSE and STOREHOUSES**. That way it shouldn't be up for speculation as to what the **STORE or STOREHOUSE** was used for.

SCRIPTURAL REFERENCES TO STORE AND STOREHOUSE

GENESIS	*26:14*
	41:36, 56
LEVITICUS	*25:22*
	26:10
DEUTERONOMY	*28:5,8,17*
	32:24

1ST KINGS	9:19
1ST KINGS	10:10
2ND KINGS	20:17
1ST CHRONICLES	27:25 29:16
2ND CHRONICLES	8:4,6 11:11 16:4 17:12 31:10 32:28
PSALMS	33:7 144:13
ISAIAH	39:6
JEREMIAH	50:26
AMOS	3:10
NAHUM	2:9
MALACHI	3:10
LUKE	12:24
1ST CORINTHIANS	16:2
1ST TIMOTHY	6:19
2ND PETER	3.7

With the above references, there is no reason to guess as to what is meant by *STOREHOUSE or STORE*; or, what was placed in them.

Jesus talked about the **storehouse** when He said:

Consider the ravens For they neither sow nor reap; which neither have storehouses nor barns; and God feedeth them: how much more are ye better than the fowls? (Luke 12:24, KJV).

Jesus has made it very clear that **storehouses** are buildings where processed food, not **money**, was stored (flour, cured meat, canned food, etc.). Unprocessed food was stored in barns (corn, wheat, live animals etc.). What reason will a raven (a bird) have to store money? *"Neither sow nor reap"* refer to planting and harvesting.

And if the birds (ravens), did plant, surely a **storehouse** and barn would have been in order. But, since they planted not, they reaped not. We can say for certain, **storehouses** were places where food was stored so the priests would have food throughout the year.

Some will say, without support of the scripture, that food was mentioned because they had no **money** in those days. Don't believe that. To say people of the Bible had no **money** does not make it so. In fact, it is not so. It is merely an opinion, which we all have. I challenge you to turn to **Genesis 13:2** and read that *"Abram [was] very rich in CATTLE, in SILVER, and in GOLD."* In fact, as early as **Genesis 2:11**, **GOLD** is mentioned. If Adam and Eve had **money** in **Genesis, second chapter**, it was available to all others also.

The abundance of **money (gold and silver)** which made Abram rich was not relegated to him alone. Many people were rich during Bible times, which can be confirmed through the scripture. If they had no **money**, people couldn't be rich in **gold** and **silver**. Please consider reference scriptures listed below which indicate the vastness of riches held by people of the Old Testament and New Testament. Scripture references are included so you might be able to read for yourself and reach your own conclusion as to whether or not **money** was or was not in supply. If people were rich and had riches, they had **money**. Just look at the amount of scripture references available in the Bible on the subject:

SCRIPTURAL REFERENCES ON THE SUBJECTS OF "RICH" AND "RICHES"

GENESIS	*13:2*
	14:23
	31:16
	36:7
EXODUS	*30:15*
LEVITICUS	*25:47*
JOSHUA	*22:8*
RUTH	*3:10*
1ST SAMUEL	*2:7*
	17:25
2ND SAMUEL	*12:1,2,4*
1ST KINGS	*3:11,13*
	10:23
1ST CHRONICLES	*29:12,28*
2ND CHRONICLES	*1:11,12*
	9:22
	17:5
	18:1
	20:25
	32:27
ESTHER	*1:4*
	5:11

JOB	15:29
	20:15
	27:19
	34:19
	36:19

PSALMS	37:16
	39:6
	45:12
	49:2,6,16
	52:7
	62:10
	73:12
	112:3
	119:14

PROVERBS	3:16
	8:18
	10:4,15,22
	11:4,16,28
	13:7
	14:20,24
	18:11,23
	19:14
	21:17
	22:1,2,4,7,16
	23:4,5
	24:4
	27:24
	28:6,11,20,22
	30:8

ECCLESIASTES	4:8
	5:12,13,14,19
	6:2
	9:11
	10:6,20

| ISAIAH | 8:4 |
| | 10:14 |

	30:6
	45:3
	53:9
	61:6
JEREMIAH	*5:27*
	9:23
	17:11
	48:36
EZEKIEL	*26:12*
	27:12,18,24,27,33
	28:4,5
DANIEL	*11:2,13,24,28*
HOSEA	*12:8*
MICAH	*6:12*
ZECHARIAH	*11:5*
MATTHEW	*13:22*
	19:23,24
	27:57
MARK	*4:19*
	10:23,24,25
	12:41
LUKE	*1:53*
	6:24
	8:14
	12:16,21
	14:12
	16:1,11,16,19,21,22
	18:23,24,25
	19:2
	21:1

ROMANS	*2:4*
	9:23
	10:12
	11:12,33
1ST CORINTHIANS	*4:8*
2ND CORINTHIANS	*6:10*
	8:2,9
EPHESIANS	*1:7,18*
	2:4,7
	3:8,16
PHILIPPIANS	*4:19*
COLOSSIANS	*1:27*
	2:2
1ST TIMOTHY	*6:9,17,18*
HEBREWS	*11:26*
JAMES	*1:10,11*
	2:5,6
	5:1,2
REVELATION	*2:9*
	3:17,18
	5:12
	6:15
	13:16
	18:3,15,17,19

Don't let any one tell you that people in the Old Testament had no **money**. How else could they be rich? If someone still insists, in light of available scripture, that **money** was not available to people in the Old or New testament, have them list all of their scriptures, as was done above, so you might see for yourself.

Avoid the conclusion that people in the Bible gave to the Sanctuary what they had, food, because they had no **money**. Such a statement is untrue. As early as the second chapter of **Genesis** it was stated that in the whole land of Havilah "**there is GOLD. And the GOLD of that land is good**" (**Genesis 2: 11-12**).

When King Solomon was in the process of building a sanctuary for God, **GOLD** was as plentiful as stones. According to the scripture *"the King made SILVER and GOLD at Jerusalem, as plenteous as stones" (2nd Chronicles 1:15, emphasis mine).* From the above reference scripture, it can't be concluded the people had no **money.** It was just the opposite, **money** was plentiful.

Some people of African American origin may relate to their own personal experience where **money** was hard to come by in years past. And in many instances in the past, African American pastors were paid with eggs, fruit, vegetation, and cured meat. The lack of **money** for this group however, had nothing to do with the lack of abundance of **money**. It had more to do with exclusion of this group from the American dream and denial of equal opportunity. Their foreparents were purchased from auction blocks, not with farm related items such as peas, corn or potatoes and okra, but with cash **money**. The **NO MONEY** theory sounds good but is without foundation.

You remember Joseph, who was sold into Egypt by his brothers? He became a great ruler there in Egypt. A great famine *"was over all the face of the earth" according to Genesis 41:56.* And Joseph opened all the **STOREHOUSES** and sold food to the people. Well, it had gotten so bad until Joseph's father, Jacob, sent his sons into Egypt from Canaan to buy **food (Genesis 43: 1-2).** How do you suppose they paid for the **food?** In **Chapter 44**, we found that Joseph tricked his brothers to make it appear they had stolen **money** to buy **food.** When questioned they gave this reply:

Behold, the MONEY, which we found in our sacks' mouths, we brought again unto thee out of the land of Canaan: How then should we steal out thy lord's house SILVER or GOLD? (Genesis 44:8, emphasis mine).

It is clear they (Joseph's brothers)had **MONEY** with them to buy needed **food**. And they didn't use **food** in place of **MONEY** because they had no **food.** If they were trading with **MONEY** in **Genesis,** how can one even suppose that they brought **FOOD** to the **STOREHOUSE** in *Malachi*, the last book in the Old Testament, because they had no **MONEY,** or, that **FOOD** in *Malachi* was used in lieu of **MONEY.** That assumption in itself, is false.

It is very important that you pay attention to the following scriptures which show, in the Bible, that the **TREASURY** was where **money** was stored. The **STOREHOUSE** was where **food** was stored. The temple had both a **TREASURE** and a **STOREHOUSE.** The Bible stated:

And over the king's TREASURES [was] Azmaveth the son of Adiel: And over the STOREHOUSES in the fields, in the cities, and in the villages, and in the castles [was] Jehonatham, the son of Uzziah (1 Chronicles 27:25, emphasis mine).

The question remains as to what was in the **TREASURY** and what was in the **STOREHOUSE**? I call your attention to the scriptures according to **Joshua**, to answer this question:

But all the silver, and gold, and vessels of brass and iron, [are] consecrated unto the Lord: They shall come into the TREASURY of the Lord (Joshua 6:19, emphasis mine).

It was made clear from the above passage of scripture that "the **TREASURY**" was where **MONEY** was stored. Now we shall see what was stored in the **STOREHOUSE.** We find in **2nd Chronicles 32:27-28**, these words:

And Hezekiah had exceeding MUCH RICHES and honor; and provided him treasuries for SILVER, and for GOLD, and for PRECIOUS STONES, and for spices, and for shields, and for all manner of goodly vessels. STORE-HOUSES also for the increase of CORN, and WINE, and OIL, and STALLS for all manner of BEASTS, and COTES for FLOCKS (emphasis mine).

Now we see the difference between **STOREHOUSES** and the **TREASURY**: **Storehouses** for **food** and **Treasuries** for **Money**. When **Malachi** talked of bringing the **TITHE** into the **STOREHOUSE**, he wasn't appealing for **money**, he was appealing for **food**. So we go back to the issue of did they have **money**? The answer, as you already know, is **YES**.

The book of **Malachi** is the last book in the Old Testament. If they had **money** in the first book, **Genesis**, don't you think they had **money** in the last book in the Old Testament (**Malachi**)? Open your Bible to **Genesis 17:23** and you will find these words:

And Abraham took Ishmael his son, and all that were born in his house, and all that were bought with his MONEY... (emphasis mine).

To prove **money** was plentiful and used in trading throughout Israel, just look at the references in the Bible pertaining to **money**:

SCRIPTURAL REFERENCES TO MONEY

GENESIS	*17:12,23,27*
	23:9,13,16
	31:15
	33:19
	42:25,27,28,35
	43:12,15,18,21-23
	44:1,2,8
	47:14,16,18

EXODUS	*12:44* *21:11,21,30,34,35* *22:7,17,25* *30:16*
LEVITICUS	*22:11* *25:37,1* *27:15,18,19*
NUMBERS	*3:48,49,50,51* *18:16*
DEUTERONOMY	*2:6,28* *14:25,26* *21:14* *23:19*
JUDGES	*5:19* *16:18* *17:4*
1ST KINGS	*21:2,6,15*
2ND KINGS	*5:26* *12:4,7-11,13,15,16* *15:20* *22:27* *23:35* *25:5,11* *34:9,14,17*
EZRA	*3:7* *7:17*
NEHEMIAH	*5:4,10,11*
ESTHER	*4:7*
JOB	*31:39* *42:11*

PSALMS	*5:5*
PROVERBS	*7:20*
ECCLESIASTES	*7:12*
	10:19
ISAIAH	*43:24*
	52:3
	55:1.2
JEREMIAH	*32:9,10,25,44*
LAMENTATIONS	*5:4*
MICAH	*3:11*
MATTHEW	*17:24,27*
	22:19
	25:18,27
	28:12,15
MARK	*6:8*
	12:41
	14:11
LUKE	*9:3*
	19:15,23
	22:5
JOHN	*2:14,15*
ACTS	*4:37*
	7:16
	8:18,20
	24:26
1ST TIMOTHY	*6:10*

It is quite clear the bartering system they used to exchange commodities was based on trading goods for **money**, not **food** in lieu of **money**.

Gold and Silver were at the base of the Hebrew or Israelite bartering system. In other words, they used **gold and silver** for **money**, the same as is used in the United States and other countries. For the record, from the books of **Genesis and Exodus** the following reference scriptures made mention of **GOLD**:

It is important to note that God made it plain and unmistakably clear of how he feels about gold. As a matter of fact, He showed John, in a vision, that the streets of heaven are paved with gold. Gold is not precious in heaven and is treated as common asphalt. Does it appear to you that God needs **money**?

After looking, John had this to report: **at the twelve gates were twelve pearls; every several gate was of one pearl: and THE STREET of the city was PURE GOLD, as it were transparent grass (Revelation 21:21).**

BIBLICAL REFERENCES ON GOLD FROM GENESIS AND EXODUS ONLY

(Too many references to include other books)

Genesis	*2:11*
	13:2
	24:22,35,53
	41:41
	44:8
Exodus	*3:22*
	11:2
	12:35
	20:23
	23:11-13,17-18,24,26,
	25:28-29,31,36,38,39
	26:6,29,32,37
	28:5,6,8,11,13-15,20,

28:22,24,26,27,33,36
30:3,5
31:4
32:24,31
35:5,22,32
36:13,34,36,38
37:2,4,6,7,11,12-33,
37:15-17,22-24,26-28
38:24
39:2,3,5,6,8,13,
39:15-17,19,25,30
40:5

From the above reference scriptures, one can easily see **money** in the form of **GOLD** was plenteous. References for **SILVER** will be listed for the entire Old Testament so you can get the full picture of how plentiful **money** was.

SCRIPTURE FROM THE ENTIRE OLD TESTAMENT ON SILVER

GENESIS	*13:2*
	23:15&16
	24:35,&53
	37:28
	44:2, & 8
	45:22
EXODUS	*3:22*
	12:35
	20:23
	21:32
	25:3
	26:19,21,25,&32
	27:10,11 & 17
	31:4
	35:5,24,&32
	36:24,26,30&36
	38:10,11,12,17,19,25&27

LEVITICUS	*5:15*
	27:3,6 & 16
NUMBERS	*7:13,19,25,31,37,*
	7:43,49,55,61,67,73
	10:2
	22:18
	24:13
	31:22
DEUTERONOMY	*7:25*
	8:13
	17:17
	22:19&29
	29:17
JOSHUA	*7:21,22,24*
	22:8
	24:32
JUDGES	*9:4*
	16:5
	17:2,3,4,10
IST SAMUEL	*2:26*
	9:8
2ND SAMUEL	*8:11*
	18:11,12
	21:4
	24:24
1ST KINGS	*7:15*
	10:21,22,25,27,29
	15:15,18
	16:24
	20:3,5,7,39
2ND KINGS	*5:5,22,23*
	6:25
	7:8

	12:13
	14:14
	15:19
	16:18
	18:14,15
	20:13
	22:4
	23:33,35
	25:15
1ST CHRONICLES	*18:10,11*
	19:6
	22:14,16
	28:15,16,17
	29:2,3,4,5,7
2ND CHRONICLES	*1:15,17*
	2:7,14
	5:1
	9:20,21,24,27
	15:18
	16:2,3
	17:11
	21:3
	24:14
	25:6,24
	27:5
	36:3
EZRA	*1:4,6,9,10,11*
	2:69
	5:15
	6:5
	7:15,16,18,22
	8:26,28,30,33
NEHEMIAH	*5:15*
	7:71,72

ESTHER	*1:6*
	3:9,11
JOB	*3:15*
	22:25
	27:16
	28:1,15
PSALMS	*12:6*
	66:10
	68:13,30
	105:37
	115:4
	119:7
	135:15
PROVERBS	*2:4*
	3:14
	8:10
	10:20
	16:16
	17:3
	22:1
	25:4,11
	26:23
	27:21
ECCLESIASTES	*2:8*
	5:10
	12:6
SONG OF SOLOMON	*1:11*
	3:10
	8:9,11
ISAIAH	*1:22*
	2:7,20
	13:17
	30:22

31:7
39:2
40:19
46:6
48:10
60:9,17

JEREMIAH	*10:4,9*
	32:9
	52:19
EZEKIEL	*7:19*
	16:13,7
	22:18,20,22
	27:12
	28:4
	38:13
DANIEL	*2:32,35,45*
	5:2,4,23
	11:8,38,43
HOSEA	*2:8*
	3:2
	8:4
	9:6
	13:2
JOEL	*3:5*
AMOS	*2:6*
	8:6
NAHUM	*2:9*
HABAKKUK	*2:19*
ZEPHANIAH	*1:11,18*
HAGGAI	*2:8*

ZECHARIAH	*6:11*
	9:3
	11:12,13
	13:9
	14:14

| *MALACHI* | *3:3* |

If the New Testament were added to the above refer-
enced list, it could be exhaustingly long. It is hard to find a
chapter in the Old Testament in which **SILVER** was not mentioned. Of the thirty-nine books in the Old Testament, thirty-
four are listed as mentioning **SILVER**. Demand any person to
show you scripture if it is claimed people in the Old Testament
used **food** for **Tithing**, because they had no **money**.

There is no question that **money** was in abundance
from early Biblical days on. The next time someone tells you
Malachi talked of bringing **Tithe** in the **Storehouse** because
the people of his day had no **money**, share the above refer-
enced scriptures with them. Be reminded people hate the bearer
of bad news. You will not become popular when you tell them
the truth. But at least the blood will not be on your hand. We
are only required to tell them the truth, not make them believe
it. Down through the ages the truth has been rejected: Even
when there is no evidence to refute it. Pride often gets in the
way, causing individuals to error to save face.

The question was asked in **2nd Kings 5:26**, *"Is it
time to receive MONEY."* God said, *"ye shall be redeemed
without MONEY (Isaiah 52:3, emphasis mine).* So during **Isaiah's** time they had **MONEY**. Even **Isaiah** asked the
question: *"Wherefore do ye spend MONEY for that which
is not bread" (Isaiah 55:2, emphasis mine).* When **Joseph**
was sold of his brothers into Egypt, do you suppose the
Ishmeelites used food for **money?** The answer is no!!

The brothers *"...sold Joseph to the Ishmeelites for
twenty (20) pieces of silver (money)" (Genesis 37:28).*

God's people were obviously rich in **silver and gold (money)**. While Moses was on the mountain of God receiving the Ten Commandments, Aaron, his brother, was in the valley making a god in the form of a calf. He didn't use food either. He used **gold** to make the calf **(Exodus 32:1-4)**. When the wise men came to visit the baby Jesus, they didn't bring food. They "...presented Him gifts; *GOLD, and frankincense and myrrh" (Matthew 2:11)*.

I can go on and on to show they had **money** from **Genesis** to **Revelations**, to give or spend. Try looking up **"money"** in the concordance of your Bible and see the many references for yourself. Look them up for yourself. **Tithe** was given in the form of food because of God's instruction, not because **money** was unavailable (more on that later). Keep in mind, it is what God said that is important. Let us go back to **Malachi 3:10**.

Next, **Malachi** said: "**...that there may be meat in mine house**" **Malachi 3:10b (KJV)**. Meat is not necessarily flesh of animals. According to *Webster's Ninth New Collegiate Dictionary*, the word "**meat**" can be described as "**the soft parts of the body of an animal. The fleshy part of a fruit.**" Fruits and vegetables constituted the meats stored in the "**house,**" not **money**. You must remember, the "**meat**" or **food** God required at His house was there to feed His priests (members of the tribe of Levi), who served Him in the Temple. The Levites had no land of their own.

Next, **Malachi** said: *And prove me now herewith, saith the Lord of hosts, if I will not open you the windows of heaven, and pour you out a blessing, that there shall not be room enough to receive it (Malachi 3:10b).*

In what way, one might ask, may the "**Windows of heaven**" be opened? The answer will be found in the book of **Genesis**, which states:

"In the six hundredth year of Noah's life, in the second month, the seventeenth day of the month, the same day were all the fountains of the great deep broken up, and the WINDOWS of heaven were opened.

"And the RAIN was upon the earth forty (40) days and forty (40) nights" (Genesis 7:11-12, emphasis mine, KJV).

We see from this scripture when the "**windows of heaven**" were opened it caused rain to fall to the Earth. The inference **Malachi** made regarding the "**windows of heaven**" in his book had the same meaning: **RAIN**, not **money**.

It is always good to try the word by the word. In the **eighth chapter of Genesis** we find these words:

The fountains also of the deep and the WINDOWS OF HEAVEN were stopped, and the RAIN from heaven was restrained (Genesis 8:2, emphasis mine).

Let us try the word by the word in confirming what is meant by "**opening the windows of Heaven**." Turn again, if you please, to **2 Kings 7:2** and you will again see the words "**WINDOWS IN HEAVEN**" because the nation of Israel was experiencing a "**famine**" (**verse 4**) and needed rain. Beware of gossip regarding the meaning of "**windows of heaven**." Search the scripture *"for in them ye think ye have eternal life" (John 5:39).*

You must not assume what is meant by the statement "**windows of heaven**" as being open or closed. You must go to the word of God. Also, you must reject what others teach as truths when the word clearly says otherwise: No matter who the teacher is. Hear the words from Paul as he writes to the **Galatians**:

But though we, or an ANGEL from heaven, preach any other gospel unto you than that which we have preached unto you, let him be accursed (Galatians 1:8, emphasis mine).

Certainly that is a powerful statement. It, in no uncertain term,highlights the importance of the word. Paul is clear in his remarks above, in that he states if an Angel brings a message from heaven that contradicts the Bible, don't believe the Angel. God and His word are the same **(John 1:1)**. Let God be true.

Believe His word, not the intellect of man. **Opening the "windows of heaven"** has absolutely nothing to do with God opening a bank and pouring you out **money**. God does not give because you gave. The Bible says:

...For He maketh his sun to rise on the evil and the good. and sendeth rain on the just and on the unjust (Matthew 5:45).

We can't trick God into blessing us by giving **money** to the church. That is lotto mentality. Because He knows what we do before we do it, and why. **Jesus said we ought to give, "hoping for nothing again, and your reward shall be great" (Luke 6:35a).** Do you want a blessing? Give from the heart and expect nothing in return. Let's not play lotto with God: That is, give a little expecting a lot in return. If your motive for giving is receiving, you have the wrong motive, according to the Bible.

When God spoke of **opening the windows of heaven**, He had reference to letting it rain and the blessings come in the form of increased crops, not **money**. God told **Malachi**:

I will rebuke the devourer (one who will destroy your crops, not your bank account) for your sakes, and he shall not destroy the FRUITS of your GROUND; neither shall your VINE cast her FRUIT before time in the FIELD, saith the Lord of hosts (Malachi 3:11, emphasis mine, KJV).

Some ministers established theories to make the above scripture refer to **money**. Vain philosophy may sound good to you, but it has no spiritual value.

Since **money** does not grow in fields or on vines, nor in the ground, we must accept the fact that God was not speaking of **money** when He spoke of "**pouring out a blessing.**" He was speaking of water, in the form of rain; rain that would be needed to grow much needed food. The point is, God was promising that if the **Tithe** was given, those who gave would not go hungry. Every time we give something from the heart to someone, and the person receiving comes into the presence of God, by way of prayer, and thanks the Lord for what you gave them, your blessing is on the way. We can't beat God giving but it must be from the heart, a **FREE WILL GIFT**.

The evidence is more than over-whelming that **Malachi 3:8-10** had absolutely nothing to do with **money**. Those who cite this scripture as a basis for teaching that God requires ten percent of our income are without foundation. Another way to put it is they are teaching a false doctrine. As a matter of fact, it is extremely unlikely that there exists a single passage anywhere in the Bible indicating God desires each of us to give Him ten percent of our paycheck.

It is true if the Bible says it. It is not necessarily true because you said it. The next time you are taught that **malachi 3:8-10** has to do with God requiring ten percent of your **money**, make the teacher show you that in the Bible. Accept no opinions, philosophies, theories, suppositions, or intellect: only the word. After all, we all have opinions.

The Apostles were given the total Gospel. If Paul told the church at **Galatia** not to accept words from an Angel sent from heaven, if that Angel's message is different from the word of God (**Gal 1:8**); surely we must reject teachings that do not line up with the word of God: Even if it sounds good and comes from an ordained minister or an educated teacher.

Malachi was not on a fund raising expedition for God as if somehow God had run short of cash in heaven: As if God couldn't make payroll and solicited his preachers and officers to glean extra owed finance for Him. When God made the earth, he placed **gold and silver** in it. Heaven was made first (**Genesis 1:1**) and God surely left much **gold** there too. Do you not know that even the streets in heaven are paved with **gold (Revelation 21:21)**. The twelve gates to the city are all made of **pearls. Malachi**, in his book, was merely pointing out where the priests had gone wrong. He was not soliciting **money** for God. Anytime God received less than the best, He is robbed.

The true interpretation of **Malachi 3:8-10** is God was merely saying to the priests, place on the altar what is proper (unblemished animals) and I will give you back more than your barns are able to hold. And to the people that brought food to the priest in the form of **Tithe**, God would open the **windows of heaven,** let it rain on their fields so that even their enemies couldn't stop their fields from increasing.

If a fraction of the time we spend at church trying to raise **money** was spent trying to witness for Jesus, the world certainly would be a better place to live and God will have the glory. I am afraid God is not happy with our action of turning His house into a crusade for **money,** not souls. I challenge anyone to find a passage of scripture where God asked someone to bring Him some **MONEY**. God wants us and when we give ourselves to Him He will automatically have our **MONEY**.

What is clear is that God desires us today to present, not our **money** to Him, but ourselves, our bodies, to Him as a living sacrifice: Dedicated totally to Him. Someone once stated that if religion was a thing that **MONEY** could buy, the rich would live and the poor would die: I agree. God wants all we have to be used to His glory, including **Money**, time, and everything else. In writing to the **Romans, Paul stated**:

I beseech you therefore brethren, by the mercies of God, that ye present your bodies a living sacrifice, holy, acceptable unto God, which is your reasonable service (Romans 12:1, emphasis mine, KJV).

God wants you. When He gets you He'll have your **money.**

In his letter to the church at Corinth, **Paul** said:

Praying us with much intreaty that we would receive the gift (money), and take upon us the fellowship of the ministering to the saints. And this they did, not as we hoped, BUT FIRST GAVE THEIR OWN SELVES TO THE LORD, and to us by the will of God (2 Corinthians 8:4-5, emphasis mine). When we give ourselves to the Lord, he will have our *money* too.

Historically, **Tithing** can be traced all the way back to Abram (Abraham) [**Genesis 14:17-21**], where King **Melchizedek** of Salem met Abram returning from battle. Abraham (Abram) had crushed the enemy of Salem and was returning with spoils. **In verse 20,** *King Melchizedek blessed Abram*. In return, Abram (whose name was later changed to Abraham), *"gave him Tithes of all" Genesis 14:20B.*

Again, we find that in **verses 21 through 24**, the King took persons and goods (not **money**). The author of **Hebrews** expounded further on this same subject in his letter to the **Hebrews** when he said (speaking of Melchizedek):

Now consider how great this man was, unto whom even the patriarch Abraham gave the tenth (meaning tithe) of the SPOILS (Hebrews 7:4 emphasis mine, KJV).

Spoils are goods taken from the enemy in battle. For a better understanding of Abraham's relationship to Levi, tribe of the Levitical priesthood, and Melchizedek, who had a relationship to Jesus, read the entire **chapter 7 of Hebrews.**

The Bible made the point that Abraham, an offspring of the tribe of Levi, paid **Tithe** to Melchizedek, who was a priest of the most high God but not a Levite. On the other hand, the **Levitical** priesthood changed (**Hebrews 7:12**) with the death of Jesus and so did the **Law of Moses** which established it in **Numbers 18:6-7.**

In placing the giving of the **tithe** by Abraham to Melchizedek in its proper perspective, it is most important to note that Abraham acted on his own will when he gave Melchizedek ten percent of his spoils. God did not instruct Abraham to give any of his spoils to Melchizedek. Nor was this the beginning of a system of giving on the part of Israel. Moreover, **Tithing**, at this time was not universal among the Hebrews. When it became time for the nation of Israel to start the process of **Tithing,** it was done according to the instruction of God, not Abraham or any other.

Jesus, according to the Bible, springs out of the tribe of Judah, a tribe of which Moses *"spake nothing concerning priesthood, and it is yet far more evidence; for that after the similitude of Melchizedek there ariseth another priest" (Hebrews 7:14-15 (KJV).*

Certainly we can say as truthful, that if the Levitical Priesthood and Moses' **Law** ended with the death of Jesus, so did **Tithing**, because universal **Tithing** was established to provide food for the tribe of Levi. This group made up the priesthood. Other provisions were made for the priests to raise needed **money** for the Sanctuary (**see Leviticus 27:1-7**). This passage too will be discussed later.

For certain, it can be stated that those who started out reading with a belief that God requires all to pay Him ten percent of their earnings must admit Biblical evidence has been presented to prove such a belief is unfounded. The Bible did not say that, and Jesus nor His apostles taught such regarding **tithing** as a requirement today.

There is not an instance in the New Testament Church, started by Jesus, where **Tithing** was taught or even mentioned as a requirement for new believers. Concerning God requiring you to give Him ten percent of your earnings, I challenge you Bible scholars to even find the word "earnings" in the Bible. I found the word "earneth" in **Haggai 1:6,** and it had nothing to do with what God required.

How did it come to this point where so many religious institutions teach and so many members believe God is requiring them to give Him ten percent of their earnings? It happened because members of these institutions didn't bother to justify or verify what they commit to belief. Many never even studied The Word of God. Others heard what was supposed to be The Word and accepted it. It is good to hear The Word. But we must try The Word by The Word. Verify The Word from what we heard. Many things we are told as gospel are nothing but what was told to the person speaking.

How should the church finance itself? This is a good question. We will get to that later. However, I will venture to say the majority of churches in America are not supported by members who **Tithe**, although many put their **money** in an envelope marked as such. Pretending to **Tithe** is un-necessary. An article appeared in the *Mobile Press Register* which showed the result of a survey on **Tithing**. Thirty nine percent of those interviewed stated they paid **Tithe**.

It is not wrong to give ten percent of your pay to the church, if in your heart that is what you wish to do. It is not wrong to give all your pay check to the church. It is wrong, however, to say God has required you to do it. Further, to teach that God will punish one for failing to give Him ten percent of his/her earnings has no scriptural support. According to the Apostle Peter, it is possible to wrestle the scripture to your own destruction (**11 Peter 3:15-16**). Find knowledge by using the method taught in **Isaiah 28:9**. And, in our teaching, if we cause others to err and stray from the faith, God will not hold us guiltless.

Indeed, in writing to the church at **Corinth** Paul reminded us we can bestow all our goods to feed the poor *"and have not charity, it profiteth me nothing" (1st Corinthians 13:3).*

It should be said however, that in the kingdom of God the value of saint is not judged by how much one accumulated while on this earth. Just the opposite, it is judged by what one gave away. In the world, the worth of a man is determined by the amount one has accumulated for himself during a lifetime. In the kingdom, what we saved gains no credits; only what we give away. Because **"it is more blessed to give than to receive" (Acts 20:35).**

However, it is the motive and spirit in which we give which determine if it were in vain or not.

CHAPTER THREE

WHAT WAS THE REQUIRED GIFT WHEN PAYING TITHE?

There is no disagreement among believers that saints of old were required to pay or give **tithe** to the Sanctuary (Hebrew Temple). What remains a topic for much discussion is what actually did this **tithe** consist of. Most will probably say that **tithe** was ten percent of the wages paid by the Israelites to keepers of the Temple. A few others probably would say the **tithe** consisted of food and food related goods Israelites were required to pay or give to the Sanctuary. What does the Bible say?

Turn, if you will, to the Book of **Leviticus, chapter 27** and **verses 30** through **34 (Leviticus 27: 30 - 34)**. These verses hold the answer to what actually constituted **tithe**. Even when reading it, many still will find reason to discount it. The Bible says:

And ALL the TITHE of the LAND, whether of the SEED of the LAND or of the FRUIT of the tree, is the Lord's: it is holy unto the Lord (vs 30, emphasis mine).

We know from this passage that **tithe** at least consisted of **FRUITS** and **VEGETABLES**. Remember, God is providing these instructions, not Moses, Abraham, or Joshua. There is no room for speculating on what constitutes the **tithe**, although some do. As we read on, from the same passage, we discover:

And concerning the tithe of the HERD, or of the FLOCK (group of animals under the guidance of a leader), even whatsoever passeth under the rod, the tenth shall be holy unto the Lord (vs 32, emphasis mine). Well, in addition to **FRUIT** and **VEGETABLES**, we see from this passage *tithe included also the* **HERD** *and the* **FLOCK** (certain animals). Again, remember we learned that **STOREHOUSES** were **"for the increase of CORN, and WINE, and OIL, and STALLS for all manner of BEASTS, and COTES for FLOCKS"** *(2 Chronicles 32:28, emphasis mine).*

From this passage of scripture we find that **Tithe** consisted of farm related products including certain animals.

Nowhere in the above passage do we see where **tithe (tenth)** constituted **money**. Remember, **Tithe** is what the Bible described it to be; not what we want it to be, or what we heard others say it is. Again, **Tithe** was food gathered from crops and farm animals, not **money** from the treasury. And since the Levites had to eat farm products given them by the eleven (11) tribes, they had to store such products in a safe place. This place where food was stored was called the **STOREHOUSE**.

We must try The Word by The Word. We must "go here a little and there a little," as was explained in **Chapter One** of this book. So let us support the above scripture from **Leviticus** with a passage of the **Book of Deuteronomy, chapter 14, verses 22 - 29:**

Thou shall truly TITHE ALL the INCREASE of thy SEED the field bringeth forth year by year (vs 22, emphasis mine).

Here again, we see that **tithe** consisted of the **SEED**. This passage gives a more descriptive view of what actually constituted **tithe**. But when we read on we find the **tithe** also included *"TITHE of thy CORN, of thy WINE, and of thine*

OIL, and the FIRSTLINGS of thy HERD and of thy FLOCK" (vs 23b, emphasis mine).

Firstlings have to do with the first born or first fruit. The **HERD** and **FLOCK**, we see again, as items that make up **TITHING**. It was the **LORD** who gave the instructions as to what was proper to offer as **tithe**. God is speaking in the above instance to Moses. How it was to be done was not for them or us to decide. Let God be true and every man a lie. Believe The Word. God took the time to explain to His people what **Tithing** was about and how He wanted it to be carried out. The action of many indicates God was wrong.

When we compare what the priest **NEHEMIAH** said, he certainly had the same understanding: That **tithes** consisted of **FRUIT** and **WINE** and everything gathered as a result of **TILLAGE, see NEHEMIAH 10:37-38**. What of those who will still say **FRUITS** and **VEGETABLES** were used because the Jews had little or no **money**? I will ask you to support that notion with scripture. However, if you just look at **NEHEMIAH 10:32** and you will see that the people made a decision to pay one third of a **SHEKEL** of **SILVER** (32 cent) **"for the service of the house of GOD"**.

Oh yes, they had **money** but it had nothing to do with their **TITHE**, a point we have made time after time. **Nehemiah** required the congregation to do both: To give a **Tithe** to the Levites so the priests could have food to eat; and give **money** for other services and needs as required in the sanctuary of the Lord **(see Nehemiah, chapter 10).** Don't bite the bait when they throw out to you the supposition that Israelites had no **money.** The Bible is the only authority on that subject.

Let us back up and stay with **NEHEMIAH** for a moment. Now turn to **chapter 13**, starting with **verse 10,** where you will see the Levites (tribe that made up the priests) leaving the temple and going to the fields because their **"portion had not been given them" (vs 10).** So **NEHEMIAH** contended with the rulers as to why those priests were in the fields and not in the Temple, as they should have been? In **chapter 13 verses 11 and 12 he stated:**

And I gathered them together, and set them in their place (their place was in the Temple). Then brought I all Judah and the TITHE of the GRAIN and the NEW WINE and the OIL unto the STOREHOUSE (vs.11 & 12, emphasis mine).

Again the scripture has been confirmed in the fact that the **TITHE** consisted of food and farm related products. **Money** was not an issue because when the people stopped bringing their **TITHES,** the priest went to work in the fields so they could have food to eat, not **money** to spend. It is evident that **money** was not consistent with **Tithing.** This point has already been made over and over again. However, this point is repeated to arm readers with scriptural references necessary to defend the truth.

Moses talked to the children of Israel about making *"an end of Tithing all the Tithes of thine increase the third year, which is the year of tithing, and hast given it unto the Levite, the stranger, the fatherless, and the widow, that they may EAT within the gates, and be filled"* *(Deuteronomy 26:12, emphasis mine).*

Go back to **Deuteronomy 14:22** and see what *"all the increase"* was. You will find it was what the field bring forth year by year; not the amount of **money** they have saved up. This is consistent with the scripture in **Deuteronomy 26:12** where the **tithe** was left the third year so the Levite and the poorer element of society could have something to **EAT** *"and be filled."* Again, they ate the **tithe** and spent the **money.**

If you go back briefly to **LEVITICUS 27,** you will see the issue of **TITHING** was covered in **verse 30** and on. However, in that same **chapter 27,** starting at the **first verse,** we see the people being taxed for **MONEY** as supported by **NEHEMIAH 10:37:**

And thy estimation shall be of the male from twenty years old, even thy estimation shall be fifty shekels of silver, after the shekel of the sanctuary. And if it be a female, then thy estimation shall be thirty shekels (Leviticus 27: 3 - 4, emphasis mine).

Read on and you will really find out how **money** for the Temple was raised. **SILVER** and **GOLD** made up the basis of their financial system **(see Jeremiah 32:9)**. They had a treasury and food was not placed in it: **Money was**. The people were taxed to support the Temple. **Money** was generated by assessing family members according to their age and gender, not with the **tithe**.

You probably have already found out that **TITHES** can be converted to **MONEY**, especially if the way was too long or for some other reason that they were not able to get to the appointed place according to the word:

And if the way be too long for thee, so that thou art not able to carry it; or if the place be too far from thee, which the Lord thy God shall choose to set his name there, when the Lord thy God hath blessed thee; then shalt thou turn it into MONEY, and bind up the MONEY in thine hand, and shalt go unto the place which the Lord thy God shall choose (DEUTERONOMY 14: 24 - 26, emphasis mine).

However, when the **TITHES** were converted from food to **MONEY**, the people were to *"Bestow that MONEY for whatsoever thy soul lusteth after" (vs. 26, emphasis mine).* If the **tithe** was **money**, how could it be converted back into **money?** You can't sell **money** (**"turn it into MONEY" [vs. 25]**). They turned food (**tithe**) into **money**.

If it were true that the people had no **money** and they gave the Temple **TITHES**, in the form of FOOD and farm products, then how could such products be converted into **MONEY?** The point being, you can't sell farm products if the people had no **money**. And, if paying **Tithe** called for giving **money**, explain how one can convert **money** into **money**. You might want to re-read **Deuteronomy 14:24-26.** For sure, we see from the scriptures the congregation had two obligations: They were required to pay **Tithes** in the form of food; and they were taxed financially for **money** needed to operate the Sanctuary of the Lord.

Some may respond that the church today does not need food. True,.the church today does not have priests to feed so food should be eliminated. However, the church today needs **money** to operate as did the church of old. **Tithing** was never instituted by the church during Bible days as a method to raise finance. God is not requiring His church today to pay **Tithe.**

CHAPTER FOUR

WHY GOD INSTRUCTED HIS PEOPLE TO PAY TITHE?

As early as the **14th chapter of Genesis** we can find the subject of **TITHE** mentioned as I stated earlier. However, **TITHING** did not become universal (all Israelites were required to do it) until they reached the promised land. You see, Jacob, who later was called Israel, had twelve sons (as recorded in **Exodus 1: 1-5**): [1] Reuben,[2] Simeon, [3] Levi (the book of Leviticus named after him), [4] Judah, [5] Issachar, [6] Zebulun, [7] Benjamin, [8] Dan, [9] Naphtali, [10] Gad, [11] Asher, and [12] Joseph. Each son became head of his tribe. Except **LEVI** (see **JOSHUA 13:33**), each tribe was given a plot of land in the promised land of Canaan.

Since this one tribe of **LEVI**, who made up the **LEVITICAL priesthood**, inherited no land, then God had to provide a way for them to eat because they were to do the service in His temple. They didn't have fields as other tribe members; therefore, there was no need for tillage and gleaning and harvesting.

Their duty was to serve the Lord in the sanctuary by offering sacrifices from the congregation.

These are the instructions God gave to Moses regarding the **Tribe of Levi** that was to serve Him in the Temple:

Behold, I have given the children of LEVI all the TENTH (which means TITHE) in Israel for an inheritance, for their service which they serve, even the service of the tabernacle of the congregation" (Numbers 18:21, emphasis mine).

God went on to say to Aaron:

But the tithes of the children of Israel, which they offer as an heave offering unto the Lord, I have given to the LEVITES to inherit: Therefore I have said unto them, among the children of Israel they shall have no inheritance" (Numbers 18:24, emphasis mine).

In applying the rule of trying The Word by The Word, we read in **Joshua 13:33** the following: **"But unto the tribe of Levi Moses gave not any inheritance: The Lord God of Israel was their inheritance."**

It is unmistakenly clear in this passage that the **TITHE** was not intended for the widows, or the poor; but for the tribe that would "**have no inheritance**" or put another way, the tribe that had no land: the Levites. Food stuff they were to receive was a reward "**for your service in the tabernacle of the congregation**" (**Numbers 18:31**). When the first census of Israel was taken, the Levites were not even counted because they were set aside for the express purpose of performing service in the Tabernacle of God (**Numbers 1:47-54**).

To get a good foundational understanding of the duties and purpose of the tribe of Levi, you need to read **chapter 18 of the book of Deuteronomy**. This chapter starts out making it clear the Levites were to have no inheritance but was to take care of the service in the temple. It was for this reason the other eleven (11) tribes were instructed to bring ten percent of their increase from the field, to the Levites in the form of **Tithes**. There is no mistake that this **Tithe** consisted of food, not ten percent of their **money**.

Well, let us assume for the purpose of discussion, that the **TITHE**, given to the Priests (or Levites), consisted of ten percentage of the earnings of the other eleven (11) tribes. They still wouldn't have continued in that office officially, after the crucifixion of Jesus. The Levitical priesthood ended when Jesus was crucified. Jesus ascended into heaven and became our high priest. There is no other high priest. Only Jesus can atone for our sins today. His blood, shed at the cross, became our ransom or payment **(Hebrews 9:12)**.

According to **Luke**, when Jesus was crucified, "**the sun was darkened and the veil of the Temple was torn in the midst**" (**Luke 23:45**). **Matthew said this**: "**The veil of the Temple was torn in two, from top to bottom...**" (**Matthew 27:51**). Even **Mark** testified to this unusual event when he wrote: "**And the veil of the Temple was torn in two, from top to the bottom**" Mark 15:38. Splitting the veil must have had an important meaning since three gospel writers thought it necessary to make mention of the event.

Well, what was the significance of the torn veil. The veil was originally meant to separate the high priest from the congregation. When an offering was given to the priests for a sacrifice, only the high priest could go into the holy place, behind the veil (**see Exodus 26:31-35**). So, when the veil was rent or torn in two (split), after the crucifixion of Jesus, it meant that service of the priests had ended. **Tithing** ended the self same moment.

Tithing was the means whereby the priests could receive food. When their service ended, so did the need to **Tithe**. The **Levitical** priesthood had no place in the atonement process after Jesus was crucified. Jesus became our mediator. His precious blood atoned for our sins, for the sins of those before us and for those who will come after.

Jesus, from that point on, became the High Priest.

The book of **Hebrews** tells us: **"We have such an High Priest, who is seated on the right hand of the throne of the Majesty, in the heavens"** (Hebrews 8:1). I tell you this High Priest is Jesus. The book went on to say: **"For we have not an high priest who cannot be touched with the feeling of our infirmities, but was in all points tempted like as we are, yet without sin. Let us therefore come boldly unto the throne of grace, that we may obtain mercy, and find grace to help in time of need"** (Hebrews 4:15-16).

So, we can conclude that even if **money** was given to the priest in the form of **TITHE** (which the scripture does not support), it would have still come to an end when Jesus was crucified, according to the scripture. The order of priesthood itself ended with the crucifixion of Jesus. Who do you think plotted the death of Jesus? It was the high priests (see **Matthew 26:1-4**). That meeting took place in the chambers of Caiaphas, the high priest. They sensed the beginning of the end of their order. They correctly blamed Jesus.

The priest would go to God for the people, in times of the Old Testament. Now we can go to God for ourselves, through Jesus. This makes us priests in our own right. Therefore the old order ended when the high priests conspired to have Jesus killed. Yes, the priests paid Judas 30 pieces of silver to deliver to them Jesus (**Matthew 26:15-16**). Peter made this remark regarding the New Testament priesthood: **"But ye are a chosen generation, A ROYAL PRIESTHOOD, an holy nation, a people of his own, that ye should show forth praises of him who hath called you out of darkness into the marvelous light"** (1 Peter 2:9, emphasis mine).

It is no small wonder that all of the apostles failed to even mention the word **TITHE**. They understood that the institution dealing with **TITHING** was no more in place.

The book of **ACTS** deals with the acts of the apostles. Surely if God intended for us to use the method of **TITHING** to raise finance for His kingdom's work, He would have revealed it to His apostles. This brings us to another point. If **TITHING** was not used to raise **money**, how did the church raise necessary **money**? And how should we today? Rest assured, these questions will be answered.

CHAPTER FIVE

HOW SHOULD CHURCHES TODAY RAISE MONEY???

From the book of **ACTS of the Apostles**(see **chapter 4:1-4**), we see the early church being perse-cuted. However, in the latter part of that chapter, we see how the needs of those less fortunate were met. Members of the church first of all were on one accord (**vs.32**). They sold their possessions and gave the church the **money**. One man by the name of Joseph was mentioned. It is stated in verses **36 and 37** that Joseph,

who by the apostles was surnamed Barnabas (which is, being interpreted, the son of consolation), a Levite of the country of Cyprus, having land, sold it, and brought the MONEY, and laid it at the apostles' feet (Acts 4:36-37, emphasis mine).

I can find no scripture showing members of the early church were required to give a certain amount. The incident listed above clearly indicated it was strictly on a voluntary basis. Further, it was their possessions to give or keep.

In **chapter 5 of Acts** we see an incident where Ananias and his wife Sapphira fell dead for not telling the truth regarding **money** made from selling land. However, Peter made it clear the profit made from the sale of land was theirs to keep when he said: **"was it not thine own? And after it was sold, was it not in thine own power...?" (Acts 5:4).**

Had Ananias told the apostles "I sold my land and I wish to give the church part of the profit," he would have told the truth and he could have avoided the wrath of God.

He went to church and acted as if he had given the church the total profit from the sale of his land. Ananias came to the church masquerading as an honest God-fearing-christian. Deception caused the wrath of God to fall on him, not the amount he gave or did not give. Clearly, his **money** was his to give or keep. The church made no demands on Ananis' **money**. That lesson is there for us today. However, many churches today are seeking lessons on giving from the antiquated, terminated formal system of **TITHING**.

When members of a church walk up before the congregation and act as if they are giving God ten percent of their income, which God has not required in the first place, they are in the exact same position as Ananias, masquerading deceit. Parading down the isles of the congregation masquerading like you have ten percent of your earnings in the envelope, when you know full well that is not the truth, is merely an exercise in deception. Even worse; those who teach or preach that God requires all to give Him ten percent of their **money**, have failed to teach the truth; have lied on God; and added to the scripture. It is written: **"If any man shall add unto these things, God shall add unto him the plagues that are written in this book" [Revelation. 22:18]**; and are in danger of kindling the wrath of God upon themselves.

In writing to the church at **Corinth** regarding collecting **money** for the saints, Paul had this to say:

Now concerning the collection for the saints, as I have given order to the churches of Galatia, even so do ye. Upon the first day of the week let every one of you lay by in store, AS GOD HATH PROSPERED HIM, that there be no gathering when I come (1 Corinthians 16:1-2, emphasis mine).

Clearly Paul wanted members to give as God had prospered them. Our instruction on giving is the exact same as Paul gave to the churches at **Galatia** and **Corinth**: free will.

It will be difficult for church members to give as God has prospered them without first giving themselves to the Lord. When God gets you, He will have your **money** also.

Paul made mention of this when he talked about how willing the saints were to give to aid those less fortunate. Speaking of giving **money**, he said:

...and this they did, not as we hoped, but first gave themselves to the Lord, and unto us by the will of God (2 Corinthians 8:5).

Listen to Paul again expound on how we in the church should give:

Every man according as he purposeth in his heart, so let him give, not grudgingly, or of necessity, for God loveth a cheerful giver" (2 Corinthians 9:7).

Read also **vs.6**. First, Paul talked about giving according **"as he purposeth in his heart:"** Not what God requires us to give him.

Second, it is clear from the above passage, if you have to give it "**grudgingly**," keep it. Why? Because "**God loves a cheerful giver.**" What about this giving "of **necessity?**" Simply put, if you necessarily need it, keep it, is what that scripture meant. God has made no demands on what you must give to Him, or what is required of you to give. It is up to the giver. What is required is that what we give be given freely and willingly.

Some of you probably know elderly people who need to buy medicine and other necessary essentials, but feel obligated to give ten percent of their entitlement check because their pastor told them God required it. Paul admonished us to give, above all, cheerfully. If you need it, keep it. Those who rush to denounce this teaching discount the scriptures.

Some treat God as they do lotto. The only reason they give is because they expect even more in return. Is this not the same reason most people play lotto? They play, expecting to win more than they played: Much, much more. God is seeking obedience, not your **money**. Even when we sacrifice and give our all, the Bible says "**...To obey is better than sacrifice**" **(1 Samuel 15:22)**. However, according to the scripture, the "**righteous showeth mercy and giveth" (Psalm 37:21)**. The righteous will always give, no matter what. Some members withhold **money** hoping to determine an outcome, wishing to create failure.

The prophet **Micah** raised the question:

Will the Lord be pleased with thousands of rams, or with ten thousand of rivers of oil? Shall I give my first-born for my transgression, the fruits of my body for the sins of my soul? He hath shown thee, O man, what is good; and what doth the Lord require of thee, but to do justly, and to love mercy, and to walk humbly with thy God? (Micah 6:7-8).

What we do for God will outweigh what we say or give. Truly if one actually had the **money** from **10,000 rivers of oil**, as mentioned in the scripture above, and gave every dollar of earned royalty to God, that wouldn't necessarily ensure anything as pertaining to spiritual dividend. Someone has said, "If religion was a thing that **money** could buy, all the rich would live and the poor would die." The **money** we claim our own is God's **money** anyway.

If one's motive for giving is to achieve self-righteousness, your giving is in vain. If in giving, you seek increased wealth, your giving is still in vain. It is when we give from the heart, expecting nothing in return, that God accepts our gifts as a blessing.

Give because it is right to give and God promised a blessing. However, a blessing may not be **money**. It could be peace of mind. It could be long life or good health. Paul stated, in a letter to the **Corinthians**:

And though I bestow all my goods to feed the poor, and though I give my body to be burned, and have not charity, it profiteth me nothing" (1 Corinthians 13:3).

Even when we give until it hurts we may still miss a blessing. Our motive for giving must be considered. The cause we give to does not make our giving righteous. Giving *"to feed the poor"* seems honorable enough but unless you had the poor at heart, your giving to them was in vain.

Back to the original issue: How should the church raise **money** needed for operation and mission. We spent time showing how food was provided for the tribe Levi. Evidence was overwhelming to indicate a universal system of **TITHING** was instituted among the various tribes, providing necessary food to the tribe of Levi. However **money** was also needed to administer the function of the Temple, the house of God. We showed the priest taxed families, by gender and age, to secure necessary funds for the Temple (**see, Leviticus 27**).

And so it was that an ordinance was passed which charged each individual within the congregation an assessment in the amount of one third part of a shekel of **silver**, as has been stated. It is recorded in the book of **Nehemiah** that such an ordinance passed that provided "**service of the house of our God**" (**Nehemiah 10:32**). The church needs **money** to operate, as did the Temple of God in times of old. The church is not powerless to raise needed **money**. It is when members are told God has required it. The local church has power.

In the Book of **Exodus**, we find God instructing Moses to tell the children of Israel to give *"a ransom for his soul unto the Lord..... This they shall give, every one that passeth among them that are numbered, half a shekel after the shekel of the sanctuary" (Exodus 30:11-13).*

It is clear that the Priests collected needed **money** by taxing the congregation. Nothing is in the scripture that prevents the church from making an assessment for the sake of determining projected needs, and thereby taxing members accordingly. In fact. it makes good sense. Not to say that is the only way. Even asking members to pay ten percent of their income is within the power of the church. But to go on and say God required them to do so is wrong. No member wishes to be out of harmony with their God. Some members will go to wits end to give what they have been told is required by God. We better be careful what we say of God.

When **Ezra** and others started to rebuild the temple of God, they needed **money,** as we do today. What did they do to get the capital? According to the book of **Ezra,**

> *some of the chief of the fathers, when they came to the house of the Lord, which sat at Jerusalem, OFFERED FREELY for the house of God to set it up in his place. They gave AFTER THEIR ABILITY unto the treasure of the work, three score and one thousand drams (one dram = $4.97) of GOLD, and five thousand pounds of SILVER, and one hundred priests garments" (Ezra 2:68-69, emphasis mine).*

As you have read, when an appeal was made for **money,** it was to be offered **FREELY.** No one was threatened by false teaching that not to give would cause God to punish them. If you read close, some of them did not give. Let the church roll on. We will always have that situation. The other point in the above passage of sripture is that the ones that gave did so according to their **ABILITY.** The key here is **free will** and **ability** to pay.

When there is truly a need and that need is properly conveyed to the congregation, the congregation likely will show faith in its leaders by responding to the call. However, to say to the congregation, "give because God has requested His **money,**" may cause members not to give to the cause. This we can say, those who fail to support the church deliberately should not be leaders in the church. Leaders lead by example. One who cannot follow leadership has no place in leading followers.

Do you wonder why **Ezra** did not appeal to the congregation and leaders to bring their **tithe** to the treasure so that necessary funds for the building of God's house would be assured? Well, because as has been stated, **tithe** was used to feed the priests, not fund them. I challenge you once to find in the Bible where **money** was needed and an appeal was made for **tithe** to secure needed funds. Yes, the church of today is empowered to collect funds necessary to carry out its mission. There are many approaches churches can use in soliciting needed funds without resorting to deliberately lying on God. A local church might seek pledges; might assess members a certain amount; might do the same for families; might establish a dues paying system; might operate from a free-will offering: But in whatever approach is used, or combination thereof, honesty should be the basis of the appeal, not deception.

Brothers and sisters, when a budget is established at the local church and members give the proposed amount, praise them. Don't make them feel guilty by saying all should have given ten percent of their earnings. If you felt that way, you should have constructed your church budget to reflect what you thought should have been given. Maybe, just maybe, if it can be justified, members will give more than ten percent of their paycheck. Where is your faith? The Bible said, **"Ask and it shall be given you" (Matthew 7:7)**.

David, King of Israel, didn't build the Sanctuary but he gathered necessary supplies, materials and funds for his son, King Solomon, to build God's first earthly sanctuary. How did he get finance and materials needed to complete the job? He certainly didn't ask for **tithes**. **Money** was donated, first by

The chief of the fathers and princes of the tribes of Israel, and captains of thousands and of hundreds, with the rulers of the King's work: OFFERED WILLINGLY. And gave for the service of the house of God, of GOLD, five thousands talents and ten thousands drams, and silver, ten thousands talents... (1 Chronicles 29:6-7, emphasis mine).

Even common people played an important role in contributing needed funds, supplies and materials toward the effort of building God a sanctuary. According to the Bible, when the congregation saw how the attitude of their leaders was regarding building God's sanctuary, *"the people rejoiced, for that they offered WILLINGLY, because with perfect heart THEY OFFERED WILLINGLY to the Lord..." (1 Chronicles 29:9, emphasis mine).*

Note: First there was a goal in mind. People didn't willingly bring of their funds, supplies and materials because someone asked. The need was pointed out and the people understood that need and agreed to support it. Their support was not out of debt they owed to God and he wanted to collect. The people saw the vision and support their leaders gave the project. That, within itself, is a lesson churches of today need to learn. Those asking others for **money** at the church should have already paid their own. Members of the finance committee should all support their church financially.

All too often, what we see is our churches who take on the mission of raising **money**. Members all too often. **MEET, GREET** and **EAT**, at the church; to raise **money**, to have a place to **MEET, GREET** and **EAT**. We all too often repeat this cycle, in the name of the Lord. All too many have accepted this limited idea as the true mission of the church. In many instances, to change such setup will either split the church or get the pastor turned off. Why? Because of the lack of teaching the true word of God. Each church, like each individual, will reap what it sows.

Giving **WILLINGLY** or **FREELY** does not prevent the local church from assessing its work and stipulating an amount members should pay in order to complete the work as planned. A great example of this is recorded in the Bible:

And the Lord spoke unto Moses, saying speak unto the children of Israel, that they bring me an offering: Of every man that giveth it WILLINGLY, with his heart, ye shall take my offering. And this is the offering which ye shall take of them, GOLD, and SILVER and BRASS (Exodus 25:1-3, emphasis mine).

Again, we see an example of a need within the congregation being met by way of taxing members. However, this assessment or tax was to be given **WILLINGLY.** Instead of conjuring up fear in the hearts of members by telling them God has required them to hand over a certain amount of **money**, based on what they make, why not use the approach described in **Exodus 25:1-3?**

If we need further examples of how the church of old raised needed funds for operation, consider this passage of scripture. God instructed Moses to tell the children of Israel, **RICH** and **POOR** alike, to give Him an offering in the amount of a half shekel of **silver**. He went on to say: *"the rich shall not give MORE, and the poor shall not give LESS" (Exodus 30:15a).* According to **verse 16** of this same chapter, **"MONEY"** was to be used for the serving of the congregation. Note: Moses was to **"tell the children of Israel,"** and from that point it was up to the congregation. It is also important to note the assessment was not based on a percentage.

If we were honest with ourselves, we will admit that **TITHING** was not the way funds were raised, either in the Old Testament or in the New Testament. And although there were different approaches, members were to give **WILLINGLY** and **FREELY.** Even when they were taxed a specified amount, it was to be given **FREELY** and **WILLINGLY.**

Scripture does not support a notion that religious leaders of old warned the congregation that not to give **money** was robbing God. God wants cheerful givers who tender their financial gifts **FREELY** and **WILLINGLY**.

Churches of today, for one thing, can establish a realistic **BUDGET** and set **GOALS** and **PRIORITIES** for each coming year. Placing a new church sanctuary in the budget just because some other church or pastor has done the same, is not realistic. Therefore members may become slack in giving when the church budget becomes unnecessarily cumbersome.

When the budget is finished by the committee within a local church, members should have an opportunity to express themselves in regards to support or lack thereof. After all, the congregation is the one who will be expected to provide the **money.** The point to be made here is you raise needed **money** by asking members to give, not misusing sacred authority telling them God will punish them if they give less than expected.

Once it was said of a church back in the country (extremely rural),that the local pastor decided it was time to pray for needed rain. After all it had not rained for six months and crops had burned up. A date was set for prayer. Members who had faith were asked to come out that night and pray for rain.

It was said that buggies, pulled by mules, were tied up long before members reached the church, indicating the large capacity of the crowd. When the pastor took to the pulpit, he simply asked one question: "All who brought their umbrellas please stand up." Needless to say, no one stood up. Therefore the pastor dismissed church on the grounds that members lacked faith. If members really believed it would rain, they would have brought their umbrellas. Such is the case with many churches regarding **tithing.** Many pastors and church leaders talk **tithing,** but when you review the budget they submit to the congregation, it does not reflect, in no way, that they had faith in what they preached.

Consider a church with 1000 members submitting an annual budget of $300,000. If 700 members paid $429 each annually, that would be more than $300,000. From this formula, church leaders evidently only calculated that 700 adult members would make less than $5,000 annually. because ten percent of $5,000 is $500 and $500 x 700 paying members = $350,000.00. Do you get the point? Why not ask members for ten percent of their income and then tell them what you expect to do with it. Just don't tell them God has demanded and commanded them to give.

Jesus left His church in the world to provide light in the world, so travelers could find their way home: That home, not made with hands, eternal in the heaven. The brightness of that light from the church is based on the amount of faith saints have in Jesus, not riches saints accumulated. Was it not Peter who told the poor beggar, *"silver and gold have I none; but such as I have give I thee: In the name of Jesus Christ of Nazareth, rise up and walk" (Acts 3:6)*. Our mission is unrelated to **money**, (see, **Matthew, 28:19-20**) but the Great Commission.

We must, as a church, throw out the lifeline and rescue the perishing; not become a repository for accumulated wealth. The church should not become a bank or some other form of savings institution. Working in the church has nothing to do with raising **money,** as some members believe. Financial drives and annual days held by many churches are unrelated to the mission of the church. Jesus spelled out the church's mission. It has not changed.

The well being of any congregation spiritually, is not based on what's in the bank, as many believe. Jesus' Great Commission as recorded in **Matthew, chapter 28, verses 19 and 20**, was not based on whether a congregation could conjure up **money**. The church can best carry out Jesus' commission by doing what He instructed us to do: **GO TEACH**, not go collect.

So then, what shall we say regarding **Tithing** to close this subject out? Give as much as you want; ten percent, twenty percent or however much. But give it from the heart. Give it willingly. Give it freely. Give it expecting nothing in return. God will bless you, not only for giving from the heart, but for whatever good you do. However, God Himself will determine how, when, and where you will get a blessing. You can't hurry God; nor can you trick God into blessing you with **money** or anything else. No one has a formula to trick God into blessing you.

Again, you can't hurry God. Support your church, in attendance, in giving and in serving. But please don't believe that God has required you to give to Him ten percent of your income. But, all you have and hope to gain already belongs to the Lord.

The scripture says **the earth is the Lord's and the fullness thereof the world and they that dwell therein.** The cattle on a thousand hills are His. All the **silver** and **gold** are His. That is why when we die we can carry nothing with us: That is, because it belongs to God. We can use it, leave it, but not have it, for keeps. What we own will follow us when we leave this earth; our deeds. Absolutely nothing else.

We came into the world with nothing and we will for certain, carry nothing out. Only our deeds will follow us. What's done and said in this life will follow us. **Money**, houses, land, cars, clothes, shoes, boats, guns and all other things, will be left behind when we die.

Who we know after we die will not matter either. It will come down to who knows us. Because if Jesus doesn't know us in the pardon of our sins, it will not really matter who else we know. Therefore, it is important that each of us gets to know Jesus. Receive Him in your life as your **LORD** and Savior, then we will be accepted in the Kingdom, where God is ruler. Spies will not even report. Going about gathering up negative information on saints will come to nothing. We can't earn our way to God, nor can we buy our way. Only by the grace of God, through Jesus Christ our Lord, can any of us expect to get to heaven.

Receive The Word: Believe The Word, and to the best of your ability live according to The Word; not because it will save you, but because you are saved. The victory will be yours.

It is written in the scriptures, that:

If thou shall confess with thy mouth the Lord Jesus, and shalt believe in thine heart that God hath raised Him from the dead, thou shalt be saved. For with the heart man believeth unto righteousness; and with the mouth confession is made unto salvation (Romans 10:9-10).

Whatever we give or did not give will not matter unless we have received Jesus. For salvation comes only from Jesus; not from what we paid or did not pay. It is finally going to come down to you and Jesus. Jesus paid the price for our salvation. **Money** was not the commodity, it was with His precious blood.

The Bible tells us a **"man that is born of a woman is of few days, and full of trouble" (Job 14:1)**. We are all here by the grace of God, no matter what the status of our health seems to be. We are all sick enough to die, this moment. As a matter of fact, all we eat contribute toward our death. Elements in all foods can cause fatality at any time. We are in the land of the dying. Eternity is the land of the living. Many have been told of being in perfect health and went home and fell dead. Others were told of serious health problems and even that death would come shortly, and lived many, many years afterward.

We who are on the earth are in the land of the dying where time is assigned to each individual. We are journeying toward the land of the living. When we get to Jesus, we will be in the land of the living.

Paul told us the last enemy to be destroyed is death **(1st Corinthians 15:26)**. When Jesus arose from the grave he declared all power was in his hand. It will be Jesus, who has all power, who will destroy death himself. According to the bible, Jesus must reign **"till He hath put all enemies under his feet. The last enemy that shall be destroyed is death. For He hath put all things under his feet" (1st Corinthians 15:25-27).**

The end will come when all things have been put under Jesus' feet, including all enemies of God. When this happens, the wicked shall cease from troubling and the weary will be at rest. God Himself, shall be with us. **"And God shall wipe away all tears from their eyes; and there shall be no more death" (Revelation 21:4-5).** If there is no more death, we will be truly and finally in the land of the living. Once we drink from the Tree of Life, we will live forever. And brothers and sisters, the frustration you may have experienced from the mouth of those who heaped for themselves, words with itching ears, full of fury, regarding giving and **tithing**, will all be over. None of this will matter when we get to glory. The former things of this world **"are passed away"** when we get home **(Revelation 21:4). HOME AT LAST, AMEN.**

CHAPTER SIX

QUICK SCRIPTURAL REFERENCES ON THE SUBJECT OF TITHING

S o much has been said regarding **Malachi 3:8-10**, in relation to **Tithing**, that I felt the necessity to list a quick reference to show the vast array of other scriptures on the subject. If one just ran the references on **Tithing** and read them I suspect your outlook would be different. Anyway, I am listing them so they will be there if you ever need them. You can tell from a quick glance the spectrum runs from **Genesis** in the Old Testament to **Hebrews** in the New Testament. To God be the Glory.

TITHING SCRIPTURES

1. GENESIS 14: 20

2. LEVITICUS 27: 30-32

3. NUMBERS 18: 24, 26, & 28

4. DEUTERONOMY 12: 6

5. DEUTERONOMY 12: 11, 12, & 17

6. DEUTERONOMY 14: 22, 23, & 28

7. DEUTERONOMY 26: 12

8. 2ND CHRONICLES 31: 5, 6, & 12

9. NEHEMIAH 10: 37, & 38

10. NEHEMIAH 12: 44

11. NEHEMIAH 13: 5, & 12

12. AMOS 4: 4

13. MALACHI 3: 8, & 10

14. MATTHEW 23: 23

15. LUKE 11: 42

16. LUKE 18: 12

17. HEBREWS 7: 5, 6, 8, & 9

It is hoped the above scriptures will serve to assist you in broadening your knowledge on the subject of **TITHING. THE END, AMEN.**

ABOUT THE AUTHOR

Is he Black or White? He feels his color is of no significance. Is he Protestant or Catholic? He feels his denominational affiliation is of no significance.

Is he a Layman of Pastor? He feels his position in the church is of no significance. Is he young or old? He feels his age is of no significance.

Is he married or single? He feels his marital status is of no significance.

Has he been educated at a recognized theological seminary? He feels his educational achievements or lack thereof are of no significance.

The author wishes his readers to know that he has placed The Word of GOD over word of mouth and the Gospel over gossip. He is acutely aware that sometimes what "mama say" is believed above what the Bible say. He has placed Christian Doctrine over any and all denominational doctrine or creeds.

This author feels to labor long on qualifications and affiliations will only provide readers an opportunity to attack the messenger and ignore the message. For this reason he has taken it upon himself to eliminate any information that would place him in conjecture with the exposition. The author wishes to be judged solely on the credibility of his work.

However, if there are comments you may wish to make regarding the content of this material, you may send them to the author's attention

P.O. Box 7931,
Mobile AL 36670.